PUPPIES

DK PUBLISHING

DK

A DK PUBLISHING BOOK

Writer and editor Carey Scott
US editor Camela Decaire
Designer Sally Geeve
DTP designer Nicky Studdart
Managing editor Linda Martin
Managing art editor Julia Harris
Production Ben Smith

First American edition, 1997
2 4 6 8 10 9 7 5 3 1
Published in the United States by DK Publishing, Inc.,
95 Madison Avenue, New York, New York 10016

Copyright © 1997 Dorling Kindersley Limited, London
Visit us on the World Wide Web at
http://www.dk.com

Published in Great Britain by Dorling Kindersley Ltd.

A catalog record for this book is available from the Library of Congress.

ISBN 0-7894-2133-X

Color reproduction by G.R.B., Italy
Printed in Italy by L.E.G.O

CONTENTS

NEWBORN PUPPIES

For two weeks after birth, puppies are completely dependent on their mother and will stay close to her, feeding and sleeping. They are born deaf and blind, but their eyes will open when they are ten to fourteen days old. Puppies can both see and hear clearly by the time they are two to three weeks old. After three weeks a puppy will start to explore, but will still need plenty of sleep. It is important that puppies are allowed to stay with their mother until they are fully developed, which takes about eight weeks.

THREE WEEKS OLD
Puppies can see, hear, and walk. They will also bark, growl, and wag their tails for the first time.

ONE WEEK OLD
At seven days old, puppies do almost nothing other than sleep and suckle. This gives them the energy they need to grow at a very fast rate.

KEEPING PUPPIES WARM
Newborn puppies are extremely susceptible to the cold until they are at least seven days old, so you may need to provide extra heating in this period. Ideally, the room temperature should be kept at around 86–91°F (30–33°C). Take care, however, not to burn puppies' delicate skin with a direct heat source.

Eyes are still firmly closed

EIGHT WEEKS OLD
Puppies are fully
developed now and can
safely leave their mothers.

SIX WEEKS OLD
A puppy's milk teeth will have
developed and he or she will be
ready to start eating small
meals.

These young
puppies are cuddled
up together for
warmth and comfort.

A muscular,
springy body
indicates a
healthy puppy.

SMALL BREEDS

The Romans were probably the first people to breed miniature dogs, and their popularity soon spread. In medieval times, people used to take little dogs to church with them to use as footwarmers! Throughout history, and in many different countries, small dogs have been the favorites of royalty. Nowadays, they are the loyal friends of lots of dog owners. However, small in size does not mean calm in nature – miniature dogs can be considerably more aggressive than large breeds.

Kyi Leo

Long hair completely covers head.

Long hair forms a veil over the eyes.

Skye Terriers

NO PROBLEM
The fluffy little Kyi Leo, originally bred in California, is easy to please. It does not need a great deal of exercise and can easily adapt to living in a small apartment.

SCOTTISH SNAPPERS
These little Terriers come from the island of Skye in Scotland, where they were bred to hunt foxes and badgers. It can take as long as three years for their silky coats to develop completely. Adult Skye Terriers make very loyal companions, but they can be snappy with children.

MEXICAN MINXES

These plucky little puppies get their name from the state of Chihuahua in Mexico, where they were first bred. The Chihuahua comes in two varieties; one with a smooth, glossy coat and one with graceful, long hair. Both varieties are sensitive to cold and tend to shiver when excited or nervous.

Pricked or erect ears are typical of this breed.

A Shorthaired and a Longhaired Chihuahua

Inquiring, intelligent expression

Yorkshire Terrier

TENACIOUS TERRIER

The Yorkshire Terrier was originally bred for miners who wanted a rat-catching dog small enough to carry in a pocket. Although the breed has retained its energetic and high-spirited nature, it still makes a loving pet.

LARGE BREEDS

There are more than 400 breeds of dogs, varying in size from the tiny 6-in (15-cm) Chihuahua to the Great Dane, which stands at 30 in (76 cm) when fully grown. Some large pedigrees have even had their size increased by careful breeding. It is important to remember that most puppies are a similar size whatever the breed. It is only later that the larger breeds start to grow at a faster rate. So, while an Irish Wolfhound pup may be comfortable in a small apartment, it will need more space as it grows. Although large dogs do not necessarily need more exercise than small ones, they do need a much larger space to run around in.

Great Danes

DIGNIFIED DANES

These wrinkly four-week-old Great Dane pups need plenty of space to exercise their growing limbs. They also have voracious appetites – an adult dog eats as much meat as a two-year-old lion. Great Danes have earned the nickname "gentle giants" because of their tolerance toward children.

St. Bernard

The Irish Wolfhound is the tallest dog in the world.

OUTDOOR PUPPY
This fluffy St. Bernard pup will keep her gentle and friendly nature as she grows up. She will make an ideal family pet provided that she is given plenty of space, exercise, and food.

Large paws indicate puppy's eventual size.

IRELAND'S PRIDE
The Irish Wolfhound, seen here with a tiny friend, is the national dog of Ireland. This ancient breed was originally used to hunt wolves. Irish Wolfhounds grow to a height of 28-35 in (71-90 cm), and make loyal companions and effective guard dogs.

Coat coloration is called harlequin.

Irish Wolfhound

AFRICAN WARRIORS
The ancestors of this pup and his dad came from the Canary Islands, off the west coast of Africa, where they were bred as fighting dogs. They have powerful, heavy bodies and massive heads.

Canary Dog and his pup

13

LONGHAIRED BREEDS

Puppies have an enormous variety of coats, from the completely hairless to the very longhaired. Breeds with long coats originated in countries with cold climates, but today long hair is encouraged by selective breeding for its appealing looks. Longhaired and fluffy puppies certainly look adorable, but do require extra care and attention. They are likely to need regular baths, and may also require special grooming to prevent their coats from becoming matted.

Bernese Mountain puppy

FROM WORKERS TO PETS

These puppies' ancestors were used to pull carts for cheese-makers and weavers in the mountains of Switzerland. Today their self-confident, happy nature makes them excellent family pets.

COLORFUL COATS

Wheaten Terrier puppies get their name from the color of their coat, which resembles ripening wheat. These cuddly, curly-haired puppies have an exceptionally cheerful and loving nature. They are very energetic and like plenty of exercise. Wheaten Terriers particularly enjoy playing, both with other animals and with children.

By kneeling on its front paws, puppy is showing it wants to play.

Soft-Coated Wheaten Terrier

SHAGGY SHEEPDOG
The Old English Sheepdog is one of England's most ancient breeds of sheepdogs. Originally bred to herd sheep and cattle, these dogs are faithful, friendly, and intelligent. This puppy's fluffy charm will soon mature into the shaggy good looks of its mom.

Old English Sheepdog

Coarse, long gray hair, with large areas of white, is typical of this breed.

UNUSUAL COATS

Some dogs are distinguished by their unique coats. The Afghan Hound's long, flowing coat, for example, makes it an extremely distinctive animal, while the Hungarian Puli has a curious "corded" coat that resembles braids. All dogs, however, are born with puppy hair – their adult coats won't develop for some time. So, be prepared for a dramatic change of appearance if you choose one of these puppies!

OUTSIZE PUPPY
An Afghan Hound starts life as a long-limbed puppy covered with short, thick fur.

Perhaps the most majestic of all dogs, the adult Afghan Hound has very long, silky hair that requires regular grooming.

Curled, slightly feathered tail is a feature of the breed.

Afghan Hound

Hungarian Puli

The adult Puli's hair hangs in long, corded strands, which makes it look rather eccentric.

WELL COVERED
Also known as the Hungarian Water Dog, the Puli has an almost waterproof coat. It is so dense that only its nose and mouth are visible beneath it. A Puli can be black, white, or apricot in color.

The coat is composed of fluffy baby hair now, but, as it grows longer, the fur will become "corded."

WOOLLY COATS

A dog's hair is made up of two distinct layers. The undercoat consists of short, soft hair, while the top coat is composed of longer, coarser hair that protects against the elements and bears the color and any pattern. This top coat can be of many different textures. Dogs with woolly coats can be fluffy or wiry. While all dogs need a certain amount of brushing, woolly breeds need either clipping or regular grooming to keep their coats in good condition.

Coat is composed of small curls and is usually a mixture of black, brown, and white.

HEROIC PETS

The fiesty Fox Terrier has a distinguished history. A Terrier named Igloo accompanied the English explorer Admiral Bird on an expedition to the Antarctic in 1928. Another Terrier, Drummer Jack, was awarded the General Service Medal for helping soldiers in World War I. Fox Terriers also make ideal pets for children. They are very energetic and love rough-and-tumble games.

Wire Fox Terrier

Long ears are set low down, wide apart, and are covered with soft, wavy hair.

FASHION FAVORITE

This Poodle puppy's ancestors came from France, where they had a variety of different roles, including retrieving ducks from water and performing in circuses. In the 1950s it became fashionable to clip a Poodle's attractive coat in a variety of styles, making the dogs stylish accessories for elegant women in cities all over the world. They have a lively, friendly nature and make loyal pets.

Poodles do not shed their curly hair, and constant growth means that it needs regular trimming. Coats can be white, gray, black, or apricot like this one.

Apricot Standard Poodle

SPORTING BREEDS

Some dogs are bred to possess the basic qualities essential for racing and hunting – speed, intelligence, and obedience. These qualities have been desirable to many dog owners for thousands of years. Although these breeds can be happy as domestic pets, they all have natural abilities that make them ideal for various sport activities.

Retrievers

Powerful muzzle and large black nose

EXPERT TRACKERS
As their name suggests, Retrievers are good at retrieving or fetching. They can easily track down small animals such as birds and rabbits. Retrievers are also powerful swimmers, and can recover game from water as well.

WILLFUL HUNTERS
A Beagle puppy may well become an avid hunter of rabbits when it is older. Beagles are known for their affectionate, happy natures, but they are also independent dogs and can have a willful streak.

Beagle

GOING FOR GAME
Cocker Spaniels are used for "flushing out" prey, particularly game birds. These dogs need plenty of exercise in order to stay fit.

Cocker Spaniel

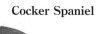

Long, elegantly
shaped head

**Italian Greyhound
and her puppies**

FAST AND FRIENDLY
Although they are capable of running up to 40 mph
(64 km/h), Greyhounds are also quite lazy and well-
suited to family life. These dainty, graceful Italian
Greyhounds were very popular in sixteenth-century
Italy, where they were kept as ladies' companions
because of their friendly, calm natures. Nowadays,
Greyhounds make loving, well-behaved, and extremely
elegant pets.

Alert ears
indicate
intelligence.

HERDING BREEDS

Human beings first domesticated the dog at least ten thousand years ago. Since then, dogs have acted as our helpers in many different ways. Their most likely career, however, is that of cattle herder, since almost every country in the world uses dogs for protecting and herding cattle. Intelligence and alertness are vital characteristics of all herding dogs, but the working method varies according to the specific skills of the breed.

Pembroke Welsh Corgi

Large, erect ears with rounded tips

LITTLE NIPPER

This ancient breed has existed in the United Kingdom since AD 920. Until the 1800s this puppy's ancestors were often used to drive cattle to market. They did this by nipping at the heels of cattle, which kept the animals in line. This earned Corgis the name "heelers."

Coat can be speckled in red or blue, or may be one color only.

OUTBACKERS
Like Corgis, these herding dogs are heelers, but are also capable of driving cattle over the long distances of the Australian outback.

Head is broad and strong and the jaw is exceptionally powerful.

Eyes set wide apart over narrowing, rather blunt muzzle

Australian Cattle puppies

Border Collie

CAPABLE COLLIE
This puppy belongs to the most famous sheepdog breed in the world. It can be trained to respond to a master's every call and whistle, and its sense of smell is so good that it can seek out and rescue a lamb that has been buried in the snow.

WORKING BREEDS

Many puppies are capable of growing up to be intelligent workers, often performing tasks that human beings cannot. Throughout history, dogs have helped people in many ways – pulling and carrying loads, acting as guards and sentries, and using their powerful sense of smell to detect anything from gas leaks to sought-after truffles.

Adult Labradors can act as a "seeing-eye" for the blind.

INVALUABLE HELPMATES

The German government was the first to take advantage of a Labrador puppy's especially affectionate and obedient nature. It trained Labradors as guide dogs for soldiers who had lost their sight in World War I. Now Labradors help blind and deaf people all over the world.

Labrador Retrievers

Coat can be black, brown, or golden. Hair is always short, dense, and waterproof.

Straight, powerful forelegs

POLICE PUPPY

This fluffy Alsatian puppy has an assertive character that will make it good at protecting both people and property when it grows up. Alsatians are also very helpful to the police, assisting them in tracking criminals and finding drugs and explosives at airports.

Adult coat is coarse, with thick undercoat.

Soft, fluffy coat will grow longer as puppy matures.

Head is broad and well-proportioned.

Deep, wide chest and powerful, level back

Alsatian, or German Shepherd Dog

MOUNTAIN RESCUE

This breed gets its name from the Great Saint Bernard Pass in the Swiss Alps, where St. Bernards were trained by monks to rescue people trapped in the snow. The most successful dog was named Barry and had rescued 40 people by the time he died in 1814.

St. Bernards

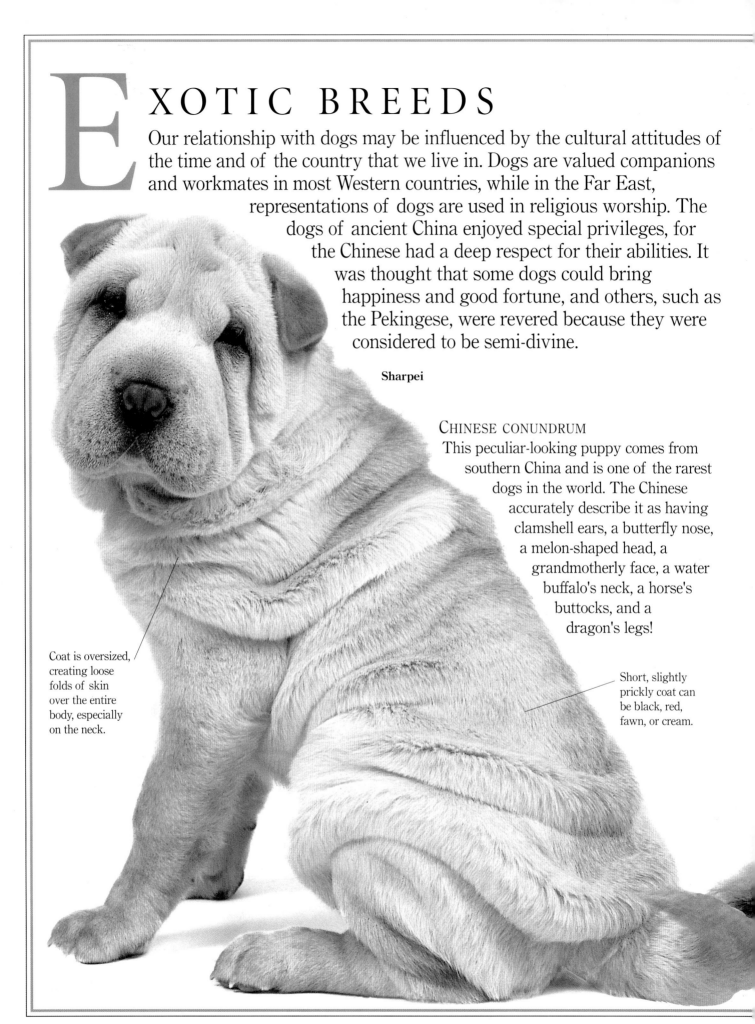

EXOTIC BREEDS

Our relationship with dogs may be influenced by the cultural attitudes of the time and of the country that we live in. Dogs are valued companions and workmates in most Western countries, while in the Far East, representations of dogs are used in religious worship. The dogs of ancient China enjoyed special privileges, for the Chinese had a deep respect for their abilities. It was thought that some dogs could bring happiness and good fortune, and others, such as the Pekingese, were revered because they were considered to be semi-divine.

Sharpei

CHINESE CONUNDRUM
This peculiar-looking puppy comes from southern China and is one of the rarest dogs in the world. The Chinese accurately describe it as having clamshell ears, a butterfly nose, a melon-shaped head, a grandmotherly face, a water buffalo's neck, a horse's buttocks, and a dragon's legs!

Coat is oversized, creating loose folds of skin over the entire body, especially on the neck.

Short, slightly prickly coat can be black, red, fawn, or cream.

26

Pekingese

ARISTOCRAT OF DOGS

Chinese legend says that the Pekingese is the offspring of a lion and a monkey, for it combines the nobility of the former with the grace of the latter. Pekingese used to be called "sleeve dogs," because they were carried in Chinese courtiers' long, flowing sleeves. These little dogs were once the sacred animal of the Chinese Royal Courts. Ordinary people had to bow to them, and to steal one was an offense punishable by death!

Lionlike body is covered by a thick coat that will become longer and straighter as the puppy matures.

Long, flowing hair grows from the bridge of the nose.

Shih Tzu

FLOWER PUPPY

The Shih Tzu is sometimes called the Chrysanthemum dog because its face looks like the flower. This breed used to be a favorite of the emperors of China.

MONGREL PUPPIES

Mongrels are dogs that have interbred with each other at random, as opposed to pedigrees, which are dogs of the same breed that have been selectively bred by humans. Mongrels are easy-care dogs – they are much less likely to suffer from the various inherited medical problems that can affect pedigree dogs and they are often better-natured as well. They are also just as affectionate as pedigrees, and much less expensive.

Inquisitive, intelligent expression is signified by pert ears and bright eyes.

RAGAMUFFIN
When choosing a mongrel puppy, remember that adult size is more difficult to estimate than with a pedigree. This puppy's long legs are a good indication that it will be quite tall when fully grown.

MIXED LITTER

If you acquire a mongrel when it is still a puppy, it is unlikely that it will have any inherited behavioural difficulties. Because they are allowed to breed by natural, rather than human, selection, mongrels are often less highly strung than their pedigree counterparts.

These puppies are huddled together for warmth. Invariably the most dominant animal wriggles her way into the middle, the warmest spot.

LEARNING THROUGH PLAY

All puppies learn through play. Play teaches timing, balance, and coordination. It is how puppies learn to communicate with each other and helps determine their future social rank. These two are learning how to inhibit their bite – an important lesson that needs to be practiced between friends.

STOP THAT!

Some people believe that mongrels are calmer than pedigree dogs. All pups, though, will chew almost anything out of curiosity.

CHOOSING YOUR PUPPY

There are many factors to think about when acquiring a puppy. Pedigree or mongrel, large or small, short- or longhaired, male or female? You will want the right dog to suit your lifestyle, not just for now, but for the next ten or twelve years. When you have considered all these points and chosen a particular puppy, you will need to check that it is fit and healthy before you take it home.

Eyes should be clear and bright.

JUDGING GOOD CHARACTER

If you are selecting a puppy from a litter, it is best to choose one that is friendly and lively, but not aggressive. You will be able to judge a puppy's character quite quickly if you watch it interacting with other puppies for a while. It is also a good idea to get to know the mother of the litter if possible. She will give you a good idea of how your puppy will develop.

Nose should be cool, wet, and clean, with no sign of a cold.

Paw size is a good indication of how big your puppy will be when it grows up.

Check that
tongue and
gums are pink.

Lift ear flaps
and check that
ear canals are
dry and clean.

Coat should be
shiny and soft.

Check that
puppy is clean
under her tail.

Inspect puppy's
coat for sores,
which are a sign
of flea infestation.

Look for strong legs
with well-developed
muscles.

Tummy should
be firm, and
not swollen.

CARING FOR PUPPIES

Your new puppy will expect you to take the place of its mother, so you must learn to be a good parent. In addition to feeding and playing with it regularly, you must take care of your puppy. You should take it to the vet for a health check and first vaccinations when it is eight to ten weeks old. Also remember that while puppies are full of energy, they still need plenty of sleep and can be worn out by very long walks.

Tail held high shows interest.

PLAYING

Puppies love to chew things, so give your puppy two or three chewable toys to play with. This will keep it amused and discourage it from destroying favorite toys or household objects. Remember to remove any dangerous items, like electrical cords, from your puppy's reach.

Chew toy with braided rope specially designed to exercise puppy's jaw muscles.

A hardy plastic toy is ideal.

Puppy exercises its new teeth on a chewable toy.

SLEEPING

Having her own special place to sleep will make your puppy feel cozy and secure. If this habit is started young, your puppy will be less likely to sleep on the sofa! You can either buy a bed like this one, or make your own by cutting away one side of a sturdy box and filling it with an old blanket or cushion.

FEEDING

Dogs are omnivores, which means that they are capable of digesting vegetables, fruit, and cereals as well as meat, so a mixed diet is best for your dog. Puppies need feeding more often than adult dogs, so give yours small meals three or four times a day. When the puppy is fully grown, you can cut meals down to once or twice a day.

Always make sure your puppy has plenty of fresh water to drink.

A soft grooming brush will make puppy's coat shiny.

GROOMING

Although all puppies clean themselves, they also benefit from regular grooming. Use a brush if your puppy has long hair and a rubber grooming glove if the coat is short. Always remember to brush downward.

TRAINING PUPPIES

All dogs need some basic training for their own safety and to acquire social skills. When your puppy is three or four months old, you can start teaching it some elementary road sense. Use a firm but gentle tone of voice when giving commands, and always reward your puppy when it has done well. Never hit your puppy – if it does not obey you, it is most probably because it does not understand your instructions.

A properly trained dog should walk calmly at your side, without pulling ahead.

Give your puppy healthy treats like good-tasting vitamin tablets.

REWARDING YOUR PUPPY
Always praise your puppy when it has done well, but do not spoil it with special food too often. Reward it with affection and words of approval so that physical attention is associated with good conduct, and only use doggy treats occasionally.

Labradors love food, so give low-calorie treats to prevent a Lab pup from becoming fat.

Stretch your hand out flat toward your puppy's head.

LEARNING TO "STAY"

You can train your dog to stay sitting by repeating the word "stay" while gradually taking a few steps back. When it gets up, begin again and repeat the command until he understands you. Once your dog obeys you, praise it immediately so that it realizes it has done well. You will also need to teach your dog to heel and to stop at curbs.

Puppy sits patiently when its master gives it the "stay" command.

You and your dog must run and jump at the same time.

JUMPING THE HURDLE

If you train your puppy well, you may be able to enter it in competitions for the best-trained dog when it is older. Your puppy could also compete in dog relay races in which you will need to work as a team. There may be a local dog club in your area that organizes sponsored walks or cross-country running.

USEFUL ADDRESSES

American Society for the Prevention of Cruelty to Animals (ASPCA)
424 East 92nd Street
New York, NY 10128
Ph: (212) 876-7700

The American Kennel Club
51 Madison Avenue
New York, NY 10010
Ph: (212) 696-8200

Animal Medical Center
510 East 62nd Street
New York, NY 10021
Ph: (212) 838-8100

American Veterinary Medical Association
1931 North Meacham Road
Schaumburg, Illinois 60173
Ph: (847) 925-8070

Humane Society of the United States
2100 L Street, NW
Washington, DC 20037
Ph: (202) 452-1100

National Education for Assistance Dog Services
PO Box 213
West Boylan, Massachusetts 01583
Ph: (508) 422-9064

PHOTOGRAPHIC CREDITS

The publisher would like to thank the following for their kind permission to reproduce their photographs:

KEY: *t* top; *c* center; *b* bottom; *l* left; *r* right

Pat Doyle: 11*br*, 19, 28

Guide Dogs for The Blind Association: 24*tr*

Sally Anne Thompson, Animal Photography: *back jacket*, 22, 25*tr*, 27*tl*

Photographers:

Paul Bricknell: 36-37*b*

Jane Burton: 6*tr*, *cl*, 7*cr*, 8*tl*, *tr*, 9*tl*, *tr*, 23*r*, 29*tl*, *cr*, 36*tl*, *tr*, 37*tl*, *tr*

Michael Dunning: *jacket*, 20*bl*, 33*cl*

Dave King: 14*b*, 16*tr*

Tracy Morgan: *jacket*, *end papers*, 6*bl*, 10*l*, *b*, *tr*, 13*br*, 14*tl*, 15, 17*tr*, *b*, 21, 23*tl*, 25*tc*, 26, 27*b*, 32, 34*b*

Tim Ridley: 33*tr*

Steve Shott: *jacket*, 5, 6*tl*, 7*tr*, *cl*, *br*, 8-9*b*, 13*tl*, 20*tl*, 24-25*b*, 25*br*, 29*br*, 33*b*, 34*tr*, 35*tl*, *br*

David Ward: 16*b*, 18

Jerry Young: 6*cr*, 12*bl*, 13*tr*

INDEX